THE VERY NAUGHTY CELL

By Lily Sacks-Hubbard, LMSW

Illustrated by Taylor Barron

ISBN 979-8-218-12431-1 (paperback)

First Edition: November 2022

This paperback edition first published in 2022

For my parents (here's the book, Dad).
To my family, you are my world, especially my two Ps.
All my gratitude to my medical team—
you saved my life, twice.

Table of Contents

A Note from the Author

When I was diagnosed with breast cancer, all my professional training as a pediatric medical social worker did not feel like enough to guide my young daughter through this minefield of emotions and experiences. I recall spending hours in the library tearing up as I screened books for my child. I found helpful information, but I did not find exactly what I felt I needed at the time—a cancer story that touches on both education and emotions related to how children experience cancer impacting their lives. I hope that as you read this book with loved ones touched by cancer, you can curl up and find some comfort together.

For additional support, please see the resource section at the end of this book.

My name is Poppy.

I want to tell you about a very naughty cell.
My mom would call it the very naughty, bad,
worst cell ever, but that's a lot to say, so I
just call it the very naughty cell.

My parents told me that our bodies are made up of a gazillion tiny cells. Each cell grows a certain way and has a special job to do to keep our bodies healthy.

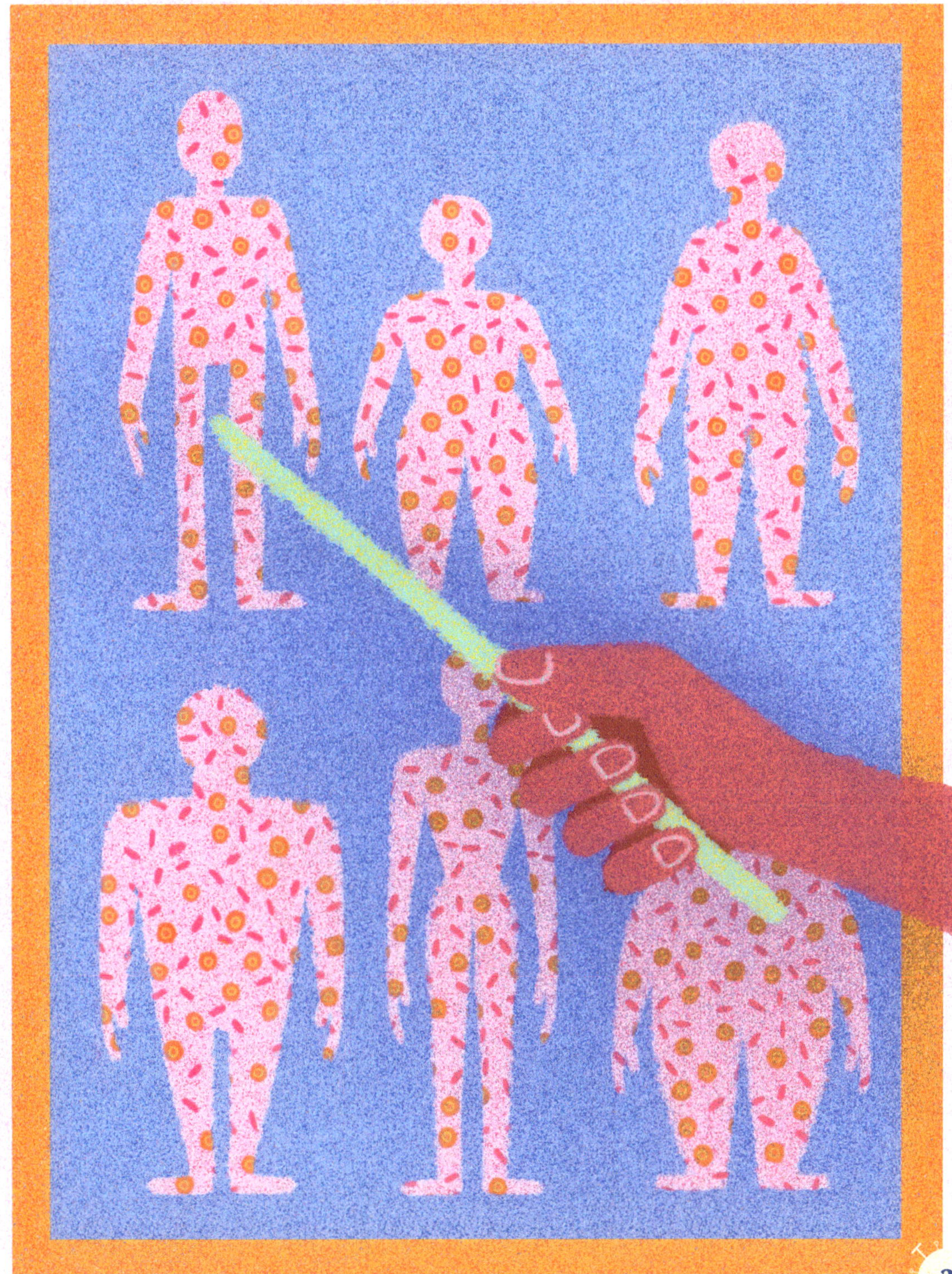

CANCER

My mom said she had cells in her body that
did not grow the right way.

They grew the very wrong way. That made
them very naughty cells. The growing wrong,
bad, very naughty cells have another name.
That name is cancer.

Cancer happens when the cells do not grow right. Cancer cells are bad for healthy bodies. My mom still looked the same and acted the same, even though she had the very naughty cells inside her. She said that I could not catch the cancer from her.

My mom was gone a lot. She got lots of
pokes for blood tests. Sometimes I got to
go with her and watch her be brave. Some
days my mom was sad and she would cry.
I would share my favorite animals and
blanket with her. This made her smile,
especially when we snuggled.

My mom needed to do lots of things with
the doctors. She was tired, but my dad and
I worked together to help her feel better.
It was hard work to be a helper, but my
mom was doing lots of hard things too.

CLAY
CLAY
CLAY
CLAY
CLAY

I went to the cancer center.
I met new friends whose
parents had cancer too.

We talked about cancer together.
We got to make clay models
of the very naughty cells.

When my mom had to do big, scary things
she would invite our friends over for dance
parties before bedtime.

We all laughed and danced. She always hugged everyone extra tight.

My mom had surgery to remove the very
naughty cells. Surgery is when the doctor
uses a special tool called a scalpel to
remove the very naughty cells. When she
came home from the hospital she slept a
lot and I could not climb on her lap.
She showed me her stitches, which looked a
little yucky but they got better fast. Then I
could snuggle on her lap again.

Surgery removed the very naughty cells, but to be super-duper sure every last cancer cell was gone she needed a medicine called chemotherapy or chemo for short.

Chemo is extra strong and good at destroying the very naughty cells. Chemo was so strong that it made my mom's hair fall out. She let me dye her hair rainbow colors. The next day we went outside and my dad and I shaved off her hair.

She looked different but I got used to seeing her with no hair. We would wear matching hats and wrap scarves on our heads.

Mom had to do one last thing called
radiation to be rid of the very naughty cells.

Radiation is an invisible force that blasts
away the very naughty cells. It made her
tired and hurt her skin.

It took a long time, but now my mom has no more of the very naughty cells in her body. My family is a little bit changed, but we are okay and I still get the best snuggles from my mom.

About the Authors

Lily Sacks-Hubbard, LMSW is a clinical social worker, two-time breast cancer patient, and parent. Lily works in pediatrics at a hospital, facilitates oncology support groups, and manages a private practice that focuses on families and cancer. She lives in Ann Arbor, MI with her daughter and husband.

Taylor Barron, is an artist and illustrator from Seattle, Washington currently living in Paris, France. She spends her time working on children's books, murals, and paintings. In her work she uses geometric forms, vibrant colors, and is passionate about exploring themes related to feminism, politics, environmentalism, and mental health.

Acknowledgments

This story would not be possible without the support, love, and generosity of so many who helped me throughout the years on this cancer journey. My circle has so much love from many—family, friends, neighbors, coworkers, and new cancer friends who came into my life.

Special thanks to my chemo crew and post-op supports who were there for the extra hard stuff. My mom, who was a near constant at our house, doing whatever needed to be done. My family, near and far, always caring and helping. The Forestbrooke love and support was invaluable. Grace Buchta, your love and care for our girl when I was unwell was the most amazing gift.

Jerry Friends and Kandy Tobias, thank you for helping make these files into an actual book. Dad, glad I made that book promise to you years ago. Dr. B. Long, Dr. K. Beekman, Dr. J. Kulick, and Dr. M.A. Kress—you are the dream team of doctors, truly.

Paul and Poppy, you two are my everything. Thanks for letting me share our story with the world to help those who are on the same journey.

In loving memory of Tori Tomalia (1976–2021)
Tori exemplified power, peace, and purpose
every day of her life.

Draw your version of Naughty Cells →

**Draw the person in your life
who has cancer** ⟶

**Draw how you are feeling in emojis.
Name and label your emojis** ⟶

Write your thoughts $\longrightarrow$

Resources

American Cancer Society: Offers programs and services to help during and after cancer treatment. Assistance with transportation to appointments, low-cost wigs, 24 hour telephone support, connection with others in treatment, and educational information.
(800) 227-2345 *https://www.cancer.org/*

Cancer Care: Provides information, one on one counseling, support groups, education programs, financial guidance, and phone support.
(800) 813-4673 *https://www.cancercare.org/*

Cancer Support Community Center: Offers support and connection with others through support groups, individual counseling, educational workshops, yoga, meditation, and nutrition classes. Family programming and support available for both children and parents.
(888) 793.9355 *https://www.cancersupportcommunity.org/*

Kids Kicking Cancer: Provides martial arts and meditation classes for children whose lives are touched by cancer. Family events and education opportunities offered.
(248) 864-8238 *https://heroescircle.org/about-us/*

National Cancer Institute: The government's primary agency for cancer research and training. Clinical trial information. Telephone support for cancer related questions.
(800)422-6237 *https://www.cancer.gov/about-cancer*